MAYOR

South Huntington Pub. Lib.
145 Pidgeon Hill Rd.
Huntington Sta., N.Y. 11746

by Jacqueline Laks Gorman

Reading consultant: Susan Nations, M.Ed., author/literacy coach/consultant

WR WEEKLY READER
EARLY LEARNING LIBRARY

Please visit our web site at: www.earlyliteracy.cc
For a free color catalog describing Weekly Reader® Early Learning Library's
list of high-quality books, call 1-877-445-5824 (USA) or 1-800-387-3178 (Canada).
Weekly Reader® Early Learning Library's fax: (414) 336-0164.

Library of Congress Cataloging-in-Publication Data

Gorman, Jacqueline Laks, 1955-
    Mayor / by Jacqueline Laks Gorman.
      p. cm. — (Our government leaders)
    Includes bibliographical references and index.
    ISBN 0-8368-4569-2 (lib. bdg.)
    ISBN 0-8368-4576-5 (softcover)
    1. Mayors—United States—Juvenile literature. I. Title. II. Series.
  JS356.G67 2005
  352.23'216'0973—dc22　　　　　　　　　　　　　2004062018

This edition first published in 2005 by
Weekly Reader® Early Learning Library
330 West Olive Street, Suite 100
Milwaukee, WI 53212 USA

Copyright © 2005 by Weekly Reader® Early Learning Library

Editor: Barbara Kiely Miller
Cover and layout design: Melissa Valuch
Photo research: Diane Laska-Swanke

Photo credits: Cover, title, © Chris Hondros/Getty Images; p. 5 © Alex Wong/Getty Images;
p. 6 © Lenny Furman/Getty Images; p. 7 © Jerry Cooke/Time & Life Pictures/Getty Images;
p. 9 © Sal Dimarco Jr./Time & Life Pictures/Getty Images; p. 10 © Stephen Chernin/Getty Images;
p. 11 © Monika Graff/Getty Images; p. 12 © Mike Simons/Getty Images; p. 13 © John Zich/Time & Life
Pictures/Getty Images; p. 15 © New York Times Co./Getty Images; p. 16 © Peter Yates/Time & Life
Pictures/Getty Images; p. 17 © Joe Raedle/Getty Images; p. 19 © Shelly Katz/Time & Life Pictures/
Getty Images; p. 20 © Julian Wasser/Getty Images; p. 21 © Todd Plitt/Getty Images

Printed in the United States of America

1 2 3 4 5 6 7 8 9 09 08 07 06 05

Cover Photo: Rudolph Giuliani was elected mayor of New York City in 1993.
          He served two terms.

TABLE OF CONTENTS

Who Are Mayors?

The United States has thousands of towns and cities. Each town or city has its own government. Many towns and cities have mayors.

A **mayor** is the head of a town or city's government. Sometimes, the mayor meets with mayors from other cities around the state. The mayor meets with people in other parts of the country, too.

Mayor Kwame Kilpatrick of Detroit, Michigan (*right*), met with members of Congress in 2003. They talked about a huge power blackout that hit much of the country that year.

In some cities, the mayor shares power with others. In Florida, Mayors Alex Penelas of Miami-Dade County (*left*) and Manuel Diaze of Miami (*right*) must work together.

Towns and cities can have different kinds of government. Some mayors have more powers than others. Some towns and cities do not have mayors at all. Groups of people run the government in these places.

A mayor lives and works in his or her town or city. A mayor's office is in a town building. In some cities, the mayor works in a building called City Hall.

Some mayors live in special houses. Some cities provide houses for their mayors. Other mayors live in their own homes.

Gracie Mansion is the official home of the mayor of New York City.

CHAPTER 2

What Does a Mayor Do?

Town and city governments perform many jobs. They may control the police and fire departments. They may run the schools and libraries. Some provide clean water and plow the snow, too. Most mayors play an important role. They make sure that all these things work well.

Many towns and cities have councils. A **council** is a group of people. The citizens of the town or city elect the people on the council. The mayor works with the council to run the town or city. The mayor may lead the meetings of the council.

W. Wilson Goode (*right*) was mayor of Philadelphia in 1985. He worked closely with the head of the city council.

In 2003, Mayor Michael Bloomberg *(seated second from left)* of New York City signed a law to fly flags over city parks.

The council passes new laws. Then the new laws go to the mayor. The mayor signs the new laws if he or she likes them. In some places, mayors do not have to sign laws that they do not like. In other places, mayors do not have this power.

Town or city governments spend a lot of money every year. The mayor may prepare the budget. The **budget** is the plan for spending the money. The mayor presents the budget to the council. The council votes to pass the budget.

New York Mayor Michael Bloomberg presented and explained the city budget in 2003.

Charlie Luken (*left*) was the mayor of Cincinnati in 2002. He signed an agreement to improve the city's police department.

A mayor makes sure that people follow the city or town's laws. Mayors work with police departments. They work with the courts. Sometimes a mayor wants a new law. He or she asks the council to pass the law.

Mayors may name the heads of town or city departments. Mayors may pick other important people in the government, too. Mayors oversee the work of many people. They also take charge when floods or tornadoes strike their towns.

A flood destroyed Valmeyer, Illinois, in 1993. The town was moved to a new location. Mayor Dennis Knobloch started the ceremony to break ground at the new location.

CHAPTER 3

How Does a Person Get to Be a Mayor?

Adult citizens of a city or town may elect the mayor. In a city with a council, sometimes the council may pick one of its members to be the mayor. When the mayor is picked by a council, he or she is often not very powerful.

Different mayors serve in their jobs for different amounts of time. A mayor's term may be only two years long. Some mayors' terms may be six years long. In some places, mayors can serve as many times as they want. In other places, mayors can serve only a few times.

Fiorello La Guardia was New York's mayor for three terms. In 1939, he met with baseball player Joe DiMaggio.

Coleman Young was mayor of Detroit from 1974 to 1994. In this picture, he is campaigning for reelection in 1989.

People who want to be elected mayor in a big city have to run big campaigns. They travel around the city. They give speeches. They run ads on TV. They have debates about their ideas.

In small towns, people who want to be mayor also run campaigns. They go to people's houses. They meet the voters.

On Election Day, citizens in the town or city vote. One candidate gets the most votes. He or she is elected mayor.

People who want to vote must first **register**, or sign up. These people are registering to vote in Miami, Florida.

CHAPTER 4

Famous Mayors

Some mayors were also elected president of the United States. Grover Cleveland was mayor of Buffalo, New York. Calvin Coolidge was mayor of Northampton, Massachusetts. They both became governors of their states. They both became president, too.

In 1973, Coleman Young was elected the first African American mayor of Detroit, Michigan. He served as mayor for twenty years. Andrew Young was mayor of Atlanta, Georgia, from 1981 to 1990. He played an important part in the fight for civil rights.

Andrew Young served as mayor of Atlanta, Georgia. He also served in other important government jobs.

Tom Bradley was mayor of Los Angeles, California. He helped unite people of many races and backgrounds.

Tom Bradley was elected mayor of Los Angeles, California, in 1973. He was the first African American mayor of the city. He was the mayor for twenty years — longer than anyone else. Mayor Bradley helped unite people. He led the city as it became the second-largest city in the country.

Rudolph Giuliani was elected mayor of New York City in 1993. He was the mayor on September 11, 2001. On that day, two hijacked airplanes attacked the World Trade Center in New York. Mayor Giuliani was a strong leader for his city. People across the country and the world admired him.

Mayor Rudolph Giuliani led New York during a terrible and scary time.

Glossary

campaigns — organized activities that people take part in to get elected

candidate — a person who seeks or is selected by others for an office or honor

citizens — official members of a place who are given certain rights, such as voting and freedom of speech. Citizens also have duties, such as paying taxes.

debates — discussions of people's different ideas and why they are for or against something

hijacked — taken over by illegal control and forced to go somewhere

natural disasters — events produced by nature that cause great damage or loss

oversee — to supervise or watch over the work of others

term — a specific period of time that a person serves in office

For More Information

Books

The City Mayor. Our Government (series). Terri Degezelle (First Facts Books)

Mayors. Community Workers (series). Alice K. Flanagan (Compass Point Books)

Rudolph Giuliani. Rookie Biographies (series). Wil Mara (Children's Press)

Web Sites

The Democracy Project
www.pbskids.org/democracy/mygovt/index.html
Find out how the government affects you, including your city government

State and Local Government on the Net
www.statelocalgov.net
A directory of government web sites where you can find your city and mayor's home pages

Index

About the Author

Jacqueline Laks Gorman is a writer and editor. She grew up in New York City. She has worked on many kinds of books and has written several children's series. She lives with her husband, David, and children, Colin and Caitlin, in DeKalb, Illinois. She always votes in every possible election.